Newport News
A Vintage Postcard Tour

*Harold N. Cones, Ph.D
and John H. Bryant, FAIA*

NN-149—Main Exhibit Room, Mariners' Museum, Newport News, Va.

3628 –Warwick County Court House, Newport News, Va.

Schiffer Publishing Ltd

4880 Lower Valley Road, Atglen, PA 19310 USA

Dedication

To LBC

Published by Schiffer Publishing Ltd.
4880 Lower Valley Road
Atglen, PA 19310
Phone: (610) 593-1777; Fax: (610) 593-2002
E-mail: Info@schifferbooks.com

For the largest selection of fine reference books on this and related subjects,
please visit our web site at **www.schifferbooks.com**
We are always looking for people to write books on new and related subjects. If
you have an idea for a book please contact us at the above address.

This book may be purchased from the publisher.
Include $3.95 for shipping.
Please try your bookstore first.
You may write for a free catalog.

In Europe, Schiffer books are distributed by
Bushwood Books
6 Marksbury Ave.
Kew Gardens
Surrey TW9 4JF England
Phone: 44 (0) 20 8392-8585; Fax: 44 (0) 20 8392-9876
E-mail: info@bushwoodbooks.co.uk
Website: www.bushwoodbooks.co.uk
Free postage in the U.K., Europe; air mail at cost.

Copyright © 2006 by Harold Cones & John Bryant
Library of Congress Control Number: 2005939179

Designed by Mark David Bowyer
Type set in ZapfChancery Mdlt BT / Korinna BT

ISBN: 0-7643-2405-5
Printed in China

Contents

Introduction

This brief introduction is an attempt to establish the groundwork necessary to enjoy the images contained in this book and to grant some measure of perspective to the several things that have defined the character of Newport News: the railroad, the shipyard, and later, the thriving community. If you are intrigued by this introduction, you may wish to refer to the bibliographic sections at its end. The sections "Further Reading About Deltiology" and "Further Reading About Newport News" contain citations of works that we have found most helpful in pursuing our own interests in these subjects.

Postcards:

What They Tell You,
How to Determine Their Age,
and How to Collect Them

• • • • • • •

March 15, 1908. *How are you getting along. It has been very hot here for the last week. With love, Agnes*

• • • • • • •

Oct. 28, 1909. *Weather perfect. Will swim today. Hope to be home for Mama's birthday Saturday. Fred*

• • • • • • •

May 16, 1908. *How are you getting along. It has been very hot for the last week, at 7:30 yesterday morning it was 85 degrees. With love, Angus*

• • • • • • •

July 16, 1907. *This is surely a nice place to visit but not to live. The weather is very hot but a stroll along shore makes things better. Love, Betty*

• • • • • • •

May 22, 1919. *Arrived here Wednesday morning from Bordeaux France. Some place down here. Expect to leave again soon for exercises. Arthur. USS Roanoke.*

• • • • • • •

From their introduction at the Chicago Columbian Exposition in 1893 until today, picture postcards have chronicled the visits and vacations of generations of travelers. The vast waters of the Chesapeake Bay, its many tributaries, and large cities, have historically attracted visitors, and, after 1893, many of these visitors sent postcards to the less fortunate "back home." Postcards with messages like those above, which were once sent from Newport News, can be found in many flea markets and antique shops. The messages are interesting, but it is the postcard front that often holds the real treasure. The postcard view freezes time, giving us a glimpse into the everyday life of people we will never know. And it was selected and sent by people who felt the occasion important enough to preserve it by sending a postcard.

Numerous postcards sent from Newport News featured cityscapes, aspects of the railroad, water activities, important buildings and, in some cases, subjects that could not have possibly been of interest to anyone. Also sent were cards from many bayside beaches, such as Buckroe Beach in Hampton, which boasted of elegant hotels, beautiful bathhouses, and, of course, thrilling amusement rides, each providing ample material for postcard views. Newport News, like Buckroe Beach had a pavilion where Big Band sounds echoed over the water on Saturday nights as couples danced to the latest rhythms. Improved highway systems, easy air travel, and changing social patterns caused many of these once proud destinations to slowly decay, but their glory survives on the fronts of postcards produced from the 1890s well into the 1960s. Postcards featured the latest in swimwear fashion, automobiles, architecture, and the things that mattered on a particular day at a particular place. And a comparison of cards through the years reveals the changes that *progress* inevitably brings.

The old Chamberlin Hotel at Fort Monroe, one of the most popular hotels on the Bay, was featured on a wide variety of postcards until it burned in a spectacular fire in March 1920. Many of these postcards prominently show the hotel, and, almost by accident, a variety of activities captured by the photographer as a consequence of the moment. These cards reveal that small boat sailing was a popular recreational activity in Hampton Roads, as it is today, as were strolls along the edge of the water, an evening outdoor band concert, or the dockside review of the Fleet. Careful study of some postcards reveals that workboats tied up at the docks eighty years ago are exactly like the workboats that fish the Bay today. The hotel, of course, is gone, but its beautiful Victorian architecture is still alive on the postcard fronts, as are the parasol-carrying ladies strolling the hotel's docks.

Do you have some old postcards lying around in a trunk somewhere and wonder just how old they are? Even if they are not postmarked, there are a few general rules of thumb that should help you date them. If the back is marked "Private Mailing Card," it was manufactured between 1898 and 1901 (usually these cards will also be marked with "Authorized by Act of Congress, May 19, 1898").

If such inscriptions are missing but the back is undivided (into address and message side), the card was produced between 1901 and 1907; these cards are usually marked "Post Card" and bear the reminder, "This Side for Address Only."

A divided back on an obviously old card, one with the picture on the front filling the entire card, dates it between 1907 and 1915. Many cards from this era were imported from Germany and England and feature stylized fine art representations of the views.

Generally, cards manufactured between 1916 and 1930 have their subject matter surrounded by a white-or-light-colored border. Because of competition and money problems, many white border era cards are of poor quality.

Cards manufactured after 1930 are known as "Linens" because of the thread-like texture of the paper on which they were printed. Linens are often surrounded by a border, but many have the image bled to the edge. These cards typically were air brushed to remove offending objects and background clutter and many linens bear a block of information on the back top left about the scene depicted on the front.

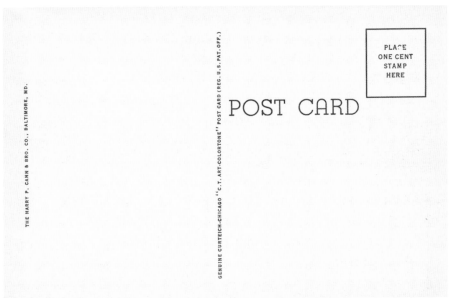

Glossy photographic-style cards were produced after 1945 and, in more recent times, "chromes" (named for Kodachrome) have been enlarged to a full 4" by 6."

One other card you may encounter is a real photo postcard. These are, as the name implies, real photographs that were printed on special postcard-size paper with a stamp block and the word "postcard" already imprinted on the back. Real photograph postcards are often one of a kind and some have information about the scene hand-etched into the negative. These cards often depict disasters such as fires, train wrecks, and ship sinkings. They can be dated by determining the manufacturer of the backing paper.

It is often helpful to examine postage stamps, if any are present. The earliest U.S. one-cent stamp used on postcards was a green frontal view of Ben Franklin that was inscribed with the years of his birth and death. In 1908, the Franklin stamp was changed to a profile and the dates were deleted. Also that year, a green one-cent profile stamp of George Washington was issued and both were in common use after 1908. Between November 1917 and July 1919, the situation is muddied a bit by the imposition of a one-cent War Tax (making postage for cards two cents). Postage for postcards increased to two cents in January 1952 and to three cents in August 1958. Postage stamps, however, are only a general indicator; often very early 1900s cards are found with two-cent stamps or with cancellations decades later than the actual period of the cards' probable manufacturing.

If you are interested in purchasing postcards, there are a number of dealers and outlets. Large, well established flea markets and antique malls may have postcard dealers and there are many on the Web; an eBay search will result in many hits. You will discover a highly volatile and often nonsensical market. Postcard pricing appears to be at the whim of the seller and you may see the same card for $.50 at one seller's booth and for $10.00 at another. Condition and cost are related and postcards are typically graded into seven categories: Mint, Near Mint, Excellent, Very Good, Good, Average and Poor. Obviously, a "Mint" card should cost more than an "Average" card, but, again, the price depends on the dealer. When faced with two cards of equal quality, we always opt for the postally used card, since the written information and date stamp provide additional information on the subject. An added benefit of the used card is that it is usually graded "Average" and therefore is less costly. Bearing in mind the nature of the market, expect to pay $1.00-15.00 for most Private Mailing Cards and less for the newer cards. What you are willing to pay for a particular card is, of course, related to your desire to have it.

The Water Front, Newport News, Va

Generic Postcards: Because of the cost of printing, it was not always possible for small towns to offer postcard views of their location. Printers responded to this need by printing large batches of general view cards and, in smaller quantities, printing the name of the town in a blank location designed into the card. These cards often bore no resemblance to the actual town, but did provide customized post cards for even the smallest town. The authors have seen the card on the right, with a different town name, from a dozen different locations. Residents of Newport News would have difficulty finding any of the locations depicted here.

Generic postcard with hand applied town name. Postmarked July 19, 1910.

Heavily embossed generic postcard.

A large-letter card was often produced by a publisher incorporating portions of a current series of postcards for the city. This card, printed in 1939, is postmarked September 21, 1948.

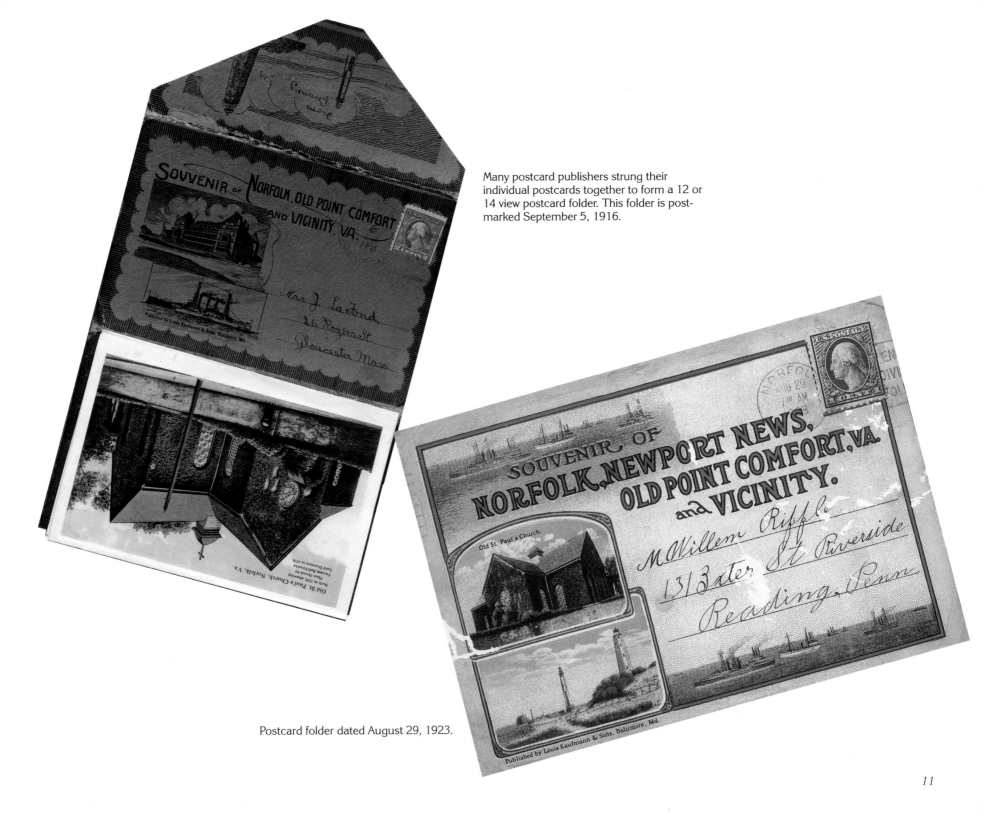

Many postcard publishers strung their individual postcards together to form a 12 or 14 view postcard folder. This folder is postmarked September 5, 1916.

Postcard folder dated August 29, 1923.

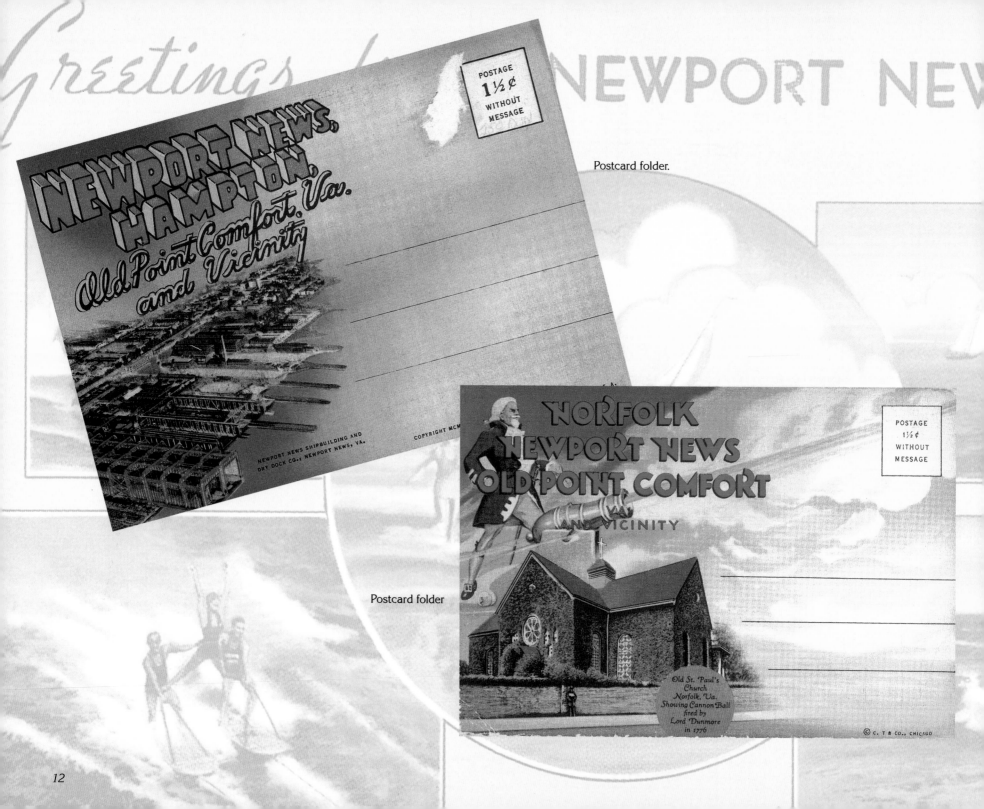

Postcard folder.

Postcard folder

Newport News Between 1607 and 1946

Newport News

Newport News: an unusual name that does not clearly speak of its derivation. There are a number of stories that explain the origin of the name, but the one most favored by the authors is a strong contender supported by existing early documentation. In 1607, Captain Christopher Newport and his flotilla of three ships touched land at Cape Charles after a very rough three and a half month voyage from England. The settlers were sent to colonize the New World for the sole purpose of making money for their underwriters, The Virginia Company. After a brief period of celebration, the colonists began a charter-mandated exploration of lower Chesapeake Bay, making the first detailed maps of the area now known as Hampton Roads. Entering a wide river, which they named the James River for King James I, the group followed the river inland and eventually chose Jamestown Island to establish a colony. The island was far enough up river to camouflage the settlement from Spanish marauders, yet close enough to the sea to allow easy passage. Captain Newport left the colonists to return to England for more settlers, leaving behind 104 people who proved to be without the skills needed to survive in the Virginia wilderness. By the next spring, half of the group had died and the remainder abandoned the settlement and followed the river to a point of land near the river's mouth, hoping to hail a passing ship. Instead they found a returning Captain Newport, with news that more ships and settlers were on their way. The legend contends that this point of land was thereafter named Newport's News. Existing documents dated 1621 and 1623 clearly state that they were written at "Newport's News."

Collis Huntington and the City to Support the Railroad

The story of the city of Newport News is the story of the Shipyard, and the story of the Shipyard is the story of Collis Potter Huntington. In 1837, Huntington saw the area that would eventually become Newport News for the first time as he passed nearby in his travels as a salesman. Subse-

quently, he settled for a time, owning a store in Oneonta, New York, but the promise of fortunes to be made in the gold fields of California sent him West in 1848. The trip to California was arduous and involved passage to Panama, crossing the isthmus by mule, and resuming the journey by ship on the other side. Huntington arrived in Panama to find the mule train passage unorganized and inefficient and to the prospects of a three-month wait for a ship to Sacramento. He bided his time by purchasing mules and instituting an efficient crossing of the country; a small boat, later resold, carried goods. By the time he left Panama, his enterprise had allowed him to increase his wealth by five times and he arrived in the gold fields financially able to establish a very successful business.

Huntington's fortune had grown to the point that by 1857 he proposed financing the Central and Pacific Railroad and planned a route across the Sierra Nevadas to the California state line. This amounted to the beginning of the first trans-continental railroad. The C&P RR was organized on April 30, 1861, with capital of $8,500,000 and the railroad was underway. By 1869, the transcontinental railroad behind him, the then famously wealthy Huntington sought to expand his railroad interests and took over the small Chesapeake and Ohio Railroad. In addition to the rails, Huntington was interested in the vast timber and coal resources found on land grants held by the C&O. The new terminus for the C&O was established at Huntington, West Virginia and Huntington began searching for a deep water terminus to offload these resources at the eastern end. The Peninsula of Virginia was an ideal spot and the Huntington group began quietly buying up land. Rural Newport News and the small town of Yorktown offered the virtue of being on protected deep water and the rumor circulated that Yorktown would be the site selected. Land speculators bought every piece of available land in Yorktown and waited as the C&O tracks came down the peninsula. As a spur slowly turned toward Yorktown, the mainline sped to Newport News Point and the announcement was made that Newport News was to be the deep water terminus of the C&O. Land speculators rushed to Newport News to find that all the land was owned by Old Dominion Land Company, Collis P. Huntington, principal officer.

There was no city of Newport News to serve the new rail terminus and, as he had done in Huntington, West Virginia, Huntington set about creating one. In 1880, the Old Dominion Land Company laid out a city with numbered streets extending east to west, starting at a point on both Hampton Roads and the James River, with avenues extending north to south named for early Virginia statesmen. The two main streets were named Washington and Lafayette (later changed to Huntington) to honor the upcoming centennial marking the anniversary of the English surrender at Yorktown. Building lots in the new city measured 25' by 100'.

Two school sites and a courthouse site were laid out and one of the first buildings in the new city was the Union Chapel, built for all faiths by the Old Dominion Land Company. In late 1880 and early 1881, deep water wharves, a coal pier, and a cargo pier were constructed on the waterfront, along with a huge grain elevator that formed a dominant part of the Newport News skyline until it was destroyed by fire (a second grain elevator, built in 1889, was also destroyed in the same fire). A pier was added for ferry service between Newport News and Norfolk in 1883. On April 11, 1883, the Warwick Hotel opened at 25th and West Avenue. In addition to providing lodging, the hotel housed the first bank, the first newspaper (*The Wedge*), the Custom's Office, a barbershop, and a drug store. In 1884, the Warwick Hotel added the Casino on the river, which housed a dance and music hall, a bowling alley, and a beach and bathhouse. A police force was also organized in 1884, and by 1887 there were three fire companies. The city of Newport News received its charter in 1886 and Walter Post became the first mayor. Citizens and Marine Bank, the area's first large bank, was organized in 1891. The *Daily Press* started publication on January 4, 1896, and Newport News claimed 42 saloons by 1900.

In 1887, D.Z. Yoder and Isaac Hertzler came to rural Warwick County, the land adjoining Newport News to the north, looking for farm land on which to establish a Mennonite Colony. The Colony quickly became known for the quality of its meats, vegetables, and dairy products sold through the Colony Farmer's Market in downtown Newport News. Oystering also proved successful, so much so that a small railroad station, Oyster Point, was opened by the C&O to handle the shipping of the large quantity of Mennonite oysters.

The Shipyard

A downturn in economics and a business depression in 1884 severely impacted the growing city. Looking to bolster the prospects of "his" city, and recognizing an ideal location, Huntington envisioned a shipyard in Newport News that would not only build boats, but provide employment for the people settling in the city. The state granted the Charter for the Chesapeake Dry Dock and Construction Company in January 1886. Three years later, Newport News Light and Water Company was chartered to provide water for the shipyard, as well as the city. Part of the water system development was the construction of Lee Hall Reservoir, chiefly to provide fire protection water for the shipyard.

Huntington moved to consolidate his business interests. He reorganized his businesses in 1889-1893 and sold much of his railroad holdings east of the Mississippi, except for those relating to Newport News. Part of the reason for this reorganization was his desire to stress ship building: the first dry dock was finished in 1889 and the first ship, Hull # 1, the tug *Dorothy*, was contracted on April 25, 1890, the same year the yard became the Newport News Shipbuilding and Dry Dock Company. As the shipyard grew, the city could not keep up with demand for housing for shipyard workers, so Huntington built 92 two-story brick row houses between 37th and 39th Streets, 46 between 36th and 37th Streets, a row of three-story houses on 27th Street, and, a row of 15 three-story houses on 28th Street for shipyard officers. Huntington also built a school primarily for the children of shipyard workers.

Homer Ferguson

Collis Huntington died in 1900, but the shipyard continued its growth and spawned another citizen who did much for the development of Newport News, Homer L. Ferguson. Ferguson became general manager of the yard in 1912 with a management style of "employees first," which was unique at the time. Ferguson encouraged homebuilding in the city and often lent the money to employees. The end of World War I resulted in a major depression and the stoppage of all military work. Under Ferguson, the yard diversified and became known for, among other things, hydraulic turbines, supplying turbines for Hoover and Grand Coolie Dams. Many years of success followed for the yard, which passed out of the Huntington family in 1940.

In 1918, Ferguson testified before a Senate Committee that the yard was unable to man a shift because of the housing shortage. With Ferguson's prodding, the first government housing project in the United States was undertaken three miles from town and named Hilton, for an old riverfront home. Planned to mimic an English village, the 500 homes and related structures of Hilton Village were placed on streets named for shipyard officials. Hilton School, completed in 1919, was placed on a riverfront lot and a trolley line connected downtown to the new project. The Colony Inn, in the Village, opened in 1927 and quickly became a focal point for the community. Hilton Village was later sold by the federal government to Henry Huntington, nephew of Collis Huntington, who offered the homes for sale for an average price of $2,800. Author William Styron grew up in Hilton Village and used aspects of the city in several of his books.

Ferguson was also very involved with the development of the Mariners' Museum and Mariners' Museum Park. Initially the project was to be a hull testing building, a model shop to build models of ships completed by the yard, and a library to house the collection of maritime books amassed by Collis Huntington's son, Archer. By 1929, the project had grown to include a maritime museum, the damming of a small creek to produce a 168-acre lake, and an 850-acre wildlife refuge. A new bridge over the new lake rerouted Route 60 from across Causey's Mill Pond to redirect it along the edge of the new park. Built in "civic proportions," the dam and lake forever changed the look of the rural Warwick County countryside. Anna Hyatt Huntington, a well known sculptor and wife of Archer Huntington, fenced a 100 acre square portion of the park to breed deer that mixed the proportions of coastal and piedmont white tail deer to provide a better specimen for her sculpting (at the conclusion of the experiment, that area was ceded to the local government and is now Deer Park). An extensive landscaping project was undertaken under the watchful eyes of Huntington and Ferguson by naturalist and shipyard hull designer George Mason. A change in tax laws stopped the further direct input of money by Huntington in 1935, but by that time, the park was essentially completed and the artifact collection was well underway.

During the development of the Mariners' Museum Park, Ferguson initiated the development of the James River Country Club by "convincing" Huntington that the area also needed the first golf museum in the United States. The Golf Museum and the Mariners' Museum share the same architecture and were landscaped at the same time by Mason, who planted live oaks from another of Huntington's estates, Brookgreen, at both locations.

Ferguson was very active in all aspects of community development, serving on many boards and giving of his time in many ways. Ferguson's wife, Elise, was also active in the community and, among a number of things, started the small facility that would eventually develop into the Peninsula Fine Arts Center. If there were ever a "first couple" in the history of Newport News, it would undoubtedly be Homer and Elise Ferguson.

Newport News at War

Newport News played a role in the Spanish American War as a troop staging area and shipping point, but its first major wartime activity occurred during World War One. Camp Stuart (between the small boat harbor and Salter's Creek) was the largest point of embarkation in the country. Two other camps developed in the area: Camp Hill, a large animal embarkation point (64th Street and the James River), and Camp Eustis, a multi-use facility. Archives are full of letters from military personnel that speak of the great hospitality shown by the citizens of Newport News to the troops stationed there. After the Armistice, the City erected a plaster and wood Victory Arch for the returning veterans; rebuilt for permanence, the Victory Arch still is a dominant feature of the downtown skyline. World War One also brought home the uniqueness of living on a peninsula with limited road access. As a result, the James River Bridge was built by a private group (encouraged by Homer Ferguson) and opened in 1928, connecting Newport News with the large manpower pool in Isle of Wight County and very soon afterwards, Norfolk and Portsmouth.

Between the Wars, Newport News prospered because of the shipyard. It was also during this time that the city became a melting pot. Large groups of European Jews, Greeks, Russians, Poles, Austrians and English came looking for work, either in the shipyard or in supporting jobs; a number of the Greeks, for example, opened restaurants near the shipyard. WNEW, the area's first radio station, went on the air in 1928 and six months later changed its call-sign to WGH (World's Greatest Harbor) and still broadcasts today as WGH. The cities first major public library, the West Avenue Library, opened in 1929.

Newport News again served as a major point of embarkation for the World War Two—1,687,000 men and women passed through the port during the War. Because of the large number of bases in the area, a military highway was constructed to connect Fort Monroe with Fort Eustis. Wartime demands for manpower at the yards and docks necessitated a number of housing projects in the early 1940s: Marshall Courts, Orcott Homes, Lassiter Courts, Stuart Gardens, Brierfield Manor, and Ferguson Park. Additionally, the nation's largest housing project—5,200 prefabricated homes—was built in Copeland Park and Newsome Park. Camp Patrick Henry (now Newport News-Williamsburg International Airport) was also developed in Warwick County as a troop staging area.

The story of World War Two in Newport News is really the story of the nation's greatest shipyard at its finest. The yard built all 49 aircraft carriers for the U.S. Navy as well as eight cruisers, eleven very large landing ships for transport (LSDs) and eighteen landing ships for tanks and other vehicles. Between 1940 and 1945, the yard additionally serviced, repaired, and converted a total of 1,597 ships. The shipyard also provided materials and labor to build recreational facilities for servicemen and local citizens throughout the War.

The history, of course, continues, though, since most postcards in this book do not postdate the World War Two, our narration will stop here.

However, two additional points need to be made: Warwick County became Warwick City in 1952 and consolidated with Newport News on July 1, 1958; and Pearl Baily, Ava Gardner, and Ella Fitzgerald at one time called Newport News home.

Postcards serve to capture the history, grandeur, and experience of a marvelous place, with productive people in a fascinating time.

Further Reading about Deltiology

Andrews, Barbara. 1975. *A Directory of Post Cards, Artists, Publishers and Trademarks*. Irving, Texas: Little Red Caboose.

Carline, Richard. 1972. *Pictures in the Post: The Story of the Picture Postcard and its Place in the History of Popular Art*. Philadelphia: Deltiologists of America.

Kaduck, John. 1975. *Mail Memories: Pictorial Guide to Postcard Collecting*. Des Moines, Iowa: Wallace-Homestead.

Smith, Jack. 1989. *Postcard Companion: The Collector's Reference*. Radner, Pennsylvania: Wallace-Homestead Book Co.

Staff, Frank. 1966. *The Picture Postcard & Its Origins*. New York: F.A. Praeger.

Further Reading about Newport News

Brown, Alexander (ed.) 1946. *Newport News' 325 Years*. Newport News: The Newport News Golden Anniversary Corporation.

Cones, Harold. 2001. *The Mariners' Museum Park: The Making of an Urban Oasis*. Newport News: The Mariners' Museum.

Evans, Cerinda. 1954. *Collis Potter Huntington*. Newport News: The Mariners' Museum.

Hawkins, Van. 1975. *A Pictorial History Hampton/Newport News*. Virginia Beach: The Donning Company.

History Commission, World War II. 1948. *Newport News During the Second World War*. Newport News: The City of Newport News.

Quarstein, John and Rouse, Jr., Park. 1996. *Newport News, A Centennial History*. Newport News: The City of Newport News.

Tazewell, William. 1986. *Newport News Shipbuilding, The First Century*. Newport News: Newport News Shipbuilding and Dry Dock Company.

Warwick River Mennonite Church. *Fifty Years Building on the Warwick*. 1947. Denbigh, VA: Warwick River Mennonite Church.

Webb, Jane. 2003. *Images of America: Newport News*. Charleston, SC: Arcadia Press.

Wheeler, Major William. 1946. *The Road to Victory, A History of Hampton Roads in World War II*. New Haven: Yale University Press.

Postmarked September 7, 1906.

Postmarked October 23, 1908.

13156. Bird's-Eye View of Newport News, Va.

C. & O. BUILDING, NEWPORT NEWS, VA. 6314

Postmarked April 11, 1910.

Newport News, Va. Chesapeake and Ohio Railway Station and Pier.

Postmarked October 21, 1910.

3631 —
C. & O.
Railroad Stat
Newport Nev
Va

SOUVENIR POST CARD CO., NEW YORK.

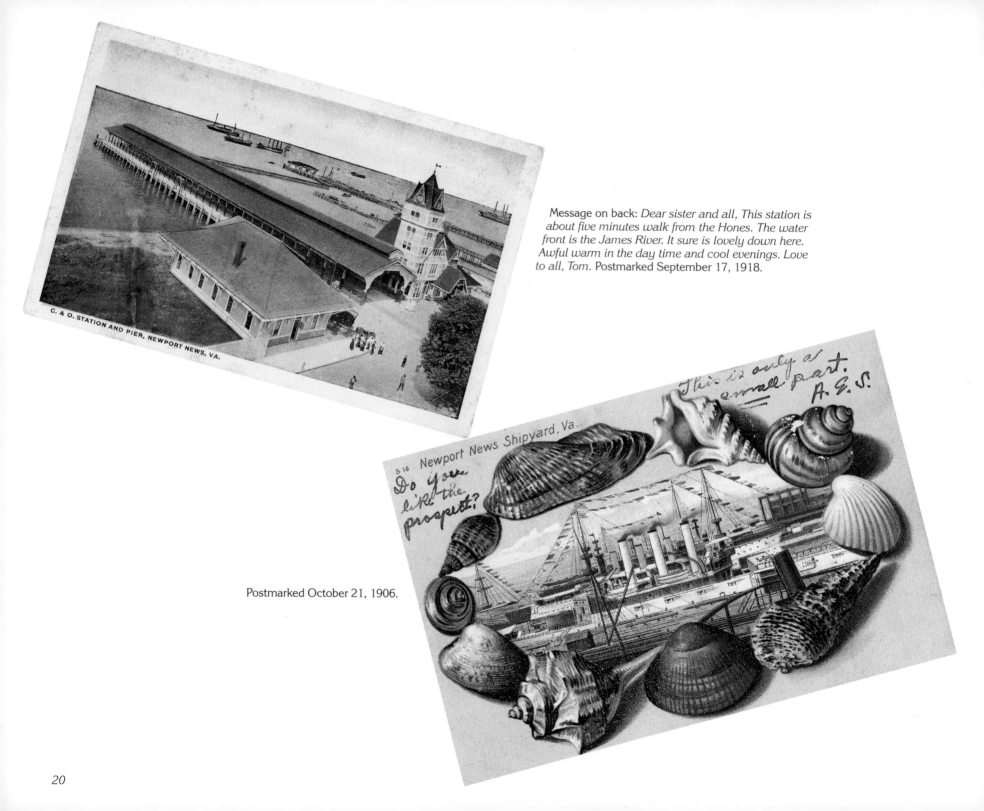

Message on back: *Dear sister and all, This station is about five minutes walk from the Hones. The water front is the James River. It sure is lovely down here. Awful warm in the day time and cool evenings. Love to all, Tom.* Postmarked September 17, 1918.

C. & O. STATION AND PIER, NEWPORT NEWS, VA.

Postmarked October 21, 1906.

Newport News Shipyard, Va.

Do you like the prospect?

This is only a small part. A. E. S.

Postmarked April 8, 1906.

Postmarked January 5, 1907.

ENTRANCE TO SHIP YARD, NEWPORT NEWS, VA.

Message on back: *Friend Lee, I suppose you have looked for a line before but my time has been taken up all the while. I am on the job every day. Like it pretty good although it is a good bit heavier and different than I have been doing. The building marked is where I work. Yours in haste, Robert.* Postmarked October 18, 1917.

3026—The largest Dry Dock in the World, accomodating 3 vessels at once, Newport News, Va.

Postmarked October 2, 1907 (Jamestown Exposition Postmark).

9122. THE GREAT DRY DOCK, NEWPORT NEWS, VA.

LARGEST DRY DOCK IN THE WORLD, NEWPORT NEWS, VA.

24

Postmarked September 21, 1904.

Postmarked May 25, 1907.

A Battleship on the Ways, prepared for Launching, Newport News, Va.

VIEW OF SHIPYARD, NEWPORT NEWS, VA.

I am spending a few days at Hotel Warwick in Newport News. Va. Hart.

Postmarked April 29, 1909.

8708. BOILER SHOP, NEWPORT NEWS SHIPYARD, NEWPORT NEWS, VA.   DETROIT PUBLISHING CO.

Postmarked March 21, 1908.

8707. SHIPYARDS AND HARBOR, NEWPORT NEWS, VA.   DETROIT PUBLISHING CO.

Postmarked December 7, 1905.

85½. SHIPPING DOCKS, NEWPORT NEWS, VA. DETROIT PUBLISHING CO.

Dear Mother: I am spending my Thanksgiving in Norfolk, Va. Hope you are well.

General View, Newport News Piers,
Newport News, Va.

Harbor and Shipping Piers, Newport News, Va.

THE C. & O. RY. CO'S. NEW COAL PIER NO. 9, NEWPORT NEWS, VA.

Newport News, Va. Glimpse of the C. and O. Coal Piers, loading Whaleback Barges.

BOAT HARBOR AND FERRY BOAT BETWEEN NORFOLK AND NEWPORT NEWS, VA.

OLD DOMINION PIER, NEWPORT NEWS, VA.

UNLOADING WATERMELONS, PIER "A," NEWPORT NEWS, VA.

Postmarked February 11, 1917.

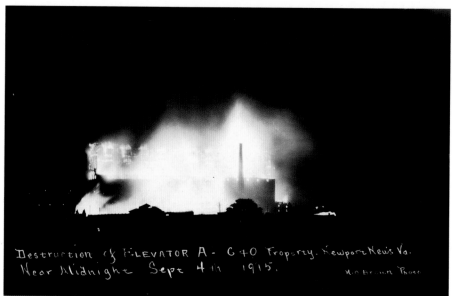

C. & O. GRAIN ELEVATOR, NEWPORT NEWS, VA.

C. & O. R.R. GRAIN ELEVATOR AND WHARVES, NEWPORT NEWS, VA.

215537

Destruction of ELEVATOR A - C & O Property. Newport News Va.
Near Midnight Sept 4th 1915.

H. D. Brown Photo

Postmarked September 10, 1915.

FOUNTAINS
BOTTLES
OLD HOMESTEAD BAKERY

BUXTON AND PARKER

EDISON PHONOGRAPHS
FACTORY PRICES. YOU SAVE THE FREIGHT
THE
ENTIRE LIST of
EDISON RECORDS.
AND ALL LATEST
ISSUES TO DATE.

IDEAL

BUXTON & PARKER FURNIT

COPYRIGHT, 1906. BY DETROIT PUBLISHING CO.

10501. TWENTY-EIGHTH STREET, NEWPORT NEWS, VA.

619   *Washington Ave, Newport News, Va.*   ILL. POST CARD CO., N.Y.

Postmarked July 27, 1905.

Postmarked September 10, 1906.

3027—View of Washington Ave. Looking North, Newport News, Va.

Souvenir Post Card Co., New York and Berlin.

Postmarked May 1, 1911.

Postmarked June 16, 1919.

WASHINGTON AVENUE, LOOKING SOUTH. NEWPORT NEWS, VA.

13158.

Washington Ave. Business Block,
Newport News, Va.

Message on back: *We were in this 5 & 10 last Friday. Dora.*
Postmarked August 11, 1911.

Washington Avenue, looking North,
Newport News, Va.

NEW WEST AVENUE RESIDENTIAL SECTION, NEWPORT NEWS, VA.

VIEW IN WARWICK PARK, NEWPORT NEWS, VA.

13166

Postmarked December 28, 1918.

West Avenue, Newport News, Va.

61349

Message on back: *June 23, 1911. Think we'll take a walk down West Avenue this morning. Won't you go with us? A.S.W.*

Newport News, Va., West Avenue, looking South.

West End Avenue, Newport News, Va.

61323

Message on back: *"Westover," 2804 West Avenue. Where we stayed from Wednesday May 4th to Thursday May 12th 1910, a beautiful spot overlooking the James River which is about 6 miles wide at this point. F.P.F."* No postmark.

BOULEVARD, NEWPORT NEWS, VA.

6328

Huntington Avenue, North End, Newport News, Va.

61300

RESIDENCES ON HUNTINGTON AVENUE AT 60TH STREET, NEWPORT NEWS, VA.

Birdseye View Newport News, Va. 1907

Bird's-Eye View, Newport News, Va., in 1887,

Postmarked July 17, 1909.

Bird's-eye View of Newport News, Va., from top of C. and O. Grain Elevator.

Birds' Eye View of Newport News, Va.

Postmarked October 1, 1906.

The Twenty Fifth Street Viaduct, Newport News, Va.

Postmarked August 6, 1907.

Postmarked March 31, 1919.

Postmarked August 17, 1908.

Stonewall Jackson School No. 5,
Newport News, Va.

STONEWALL JACKSON SCHOOL

61346

617

SILSBY BUILDING, Newport News, Va,

ILL. P. CARD CO., 118 CHAMBERS ST., N. Y.

42

ELECTRIC LIGHT PLANT, NEWPORT NEWS, VA.

Message on back: *My! But it is hot. Just sizzling. Come down and go to the seashore and see how we keep cool.* Postmarked July 19, 1911.

Postmarked April 2, 1906.

3628 —Warwick County Court House, Newport News, Va.

Court House and Jail, Newport News, Va.   *13157.*

Postmarked May 5, 1915.

Y. M. C. A. BUILDING,
NEWPORT NEWS, VA

Postmarked July 20, 1911.

Postmarked September 9, 1906.

Postmarked February 21, 1909.

West Avenue, showing Post Office, Custom House, and Hotel Warwick, Newport News, Va.

9145. GOVERNMENT BUILDING, NEWPORT NEWS, VA.   COPYRIGHT, 1905, BY DETROIT PUBLISHING CO.

Custom House and Post Office, Newport News, Va.

Postmarked October 19, 1909.

46

POST OFFICE, NEWPORT NEWS, VA. 6327

Postmarked September 9, 1907.

I. S. Post Office, Newport News, Va.   *Jamestown Exposition Grounds, Va.,*

132—Quartered Oak 133—African Mahogany
Can be furnished Hinged and Tufted Top

Exhibitors in Section 13
Manufactures and
Liberal Arts Bldg.

1907

Compliments of
NATIONAL
CASKET CO

Postmarked September 27, 1907 (Jamestown Exposition postmark).

U. S. POST OFFICE AND CUSTOM HOUSE.   NEWPORT NEWS, VA.

TRINITY METHODIST CHURCH AND WASHINGTON SQUARE, NEWPORT NEWS, VA.

Washington Square, Newport News, Va., showing
M. E. Church and Coferton Hotel.

Postmarked
September 29, 1917.

Washington Square, Newport News, Va.

GROUP OF CHURCHES

ST. PAUL'S EPISCOPAL.

FIRST BAPTIST CHURCH.

M.E. CHURCH.

NEWPORT NEWS, VA.

Postmarked June 11, 1912.

WASHINGTON SQUARE AND TRINITY M. E. CHURCH.   NEWPORT NEWS, VA.

TRINITY M. E. CHURCH,   NEWPORT NEWS, VA.

REVIVAL SERVICE

TONIGHT

Thirty-second Street showing First Presbyterian Church and Y. M. C. A., Newport News, Va.

61350

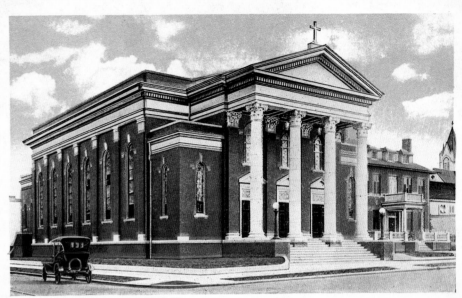

CATHOLIC CHURCH, NEWPORT NEWS, VA.

Postmarked April 18, 1919.

INTERIOR ST. VINCENT CATHOLIC CHURCH, NEWPORT NEWS, VA.

CHESTNUT STREET
25th AVE.

Chestnut Ave. Methodist Church
Welcomes You...

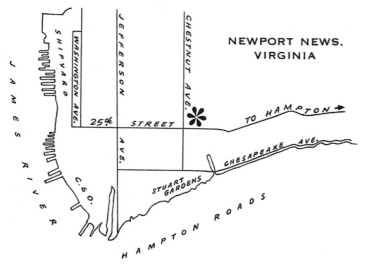

NEWPORT NEWS,
VIRGINIA

Grace Methodist Church

51st Street and Huntington Avenue

Newport News, Virginia

FIRST BAPTIST CHURCH, NEWPORT NEWS, VA.

NN-155—First Baptist Church, Newport News, Va.

6B-H1828

Elizabeth Buxton Hospital, Hampton Roads. NEWPORT NEWS, Va.

Postmarked February 21, 1913.

ELIZABETH BUXTON HOSPITAL, NEWPORT NEWS, VA.

6323

Postmarked April 17, 1913.

ELIZABETH BUXTON HOSPITAL, HAMPTON ROADS, NEWPORT NEWS, VA.

ELIZABETH BUXTON HOSPITAL, NEWPORT NEWS, VA.

WARWICK HOTEL, NEWPORT NEWS, VA.

6245. COPYRIGHT, 1902, BY DETROIT PHOTOGRAPHIC CO.

RIVERSIDE HOSPITAL, NEWPORT NEWS. VA.

Warwick Hotel, Newport News, Va.

3045.

Postmarked August 9, 1909.

Warwick Hotel and Post Office, Newport News, Va.

215540

13159. The Warwick Hotel, Newport News, Va.

Message on back: *We are still in the land of the living but not in a place I would like to* *live*. *Mrs. Bukner*. Illegible postmark.

SOUVENIR POST CARD CO., NEW YORK.

3626 — Hotel Warwick, Newport News, Va.

©Griffith Photo, Newport News, Va.

HOTEL WARWICK, NEWPORT NEWS, VA.

Applying glitter to highlight portions of postcards was popular through the 1930s. Postmarked December 1, 1906.

3030—Hotel Warwick, Newport News, Va.

I have sent you Card Willie White

Souvenir Post Card Co., New York and Berlin.

WARWICK PARK.

HOTEL WARWICK
NEWPORT NEWS
VIRGINIA.
L. B. MANVILLE
MANAGER

PARLOR

WARWICK HOTEL.

LOBBY

Hotel Warwick, Newport News, Va.

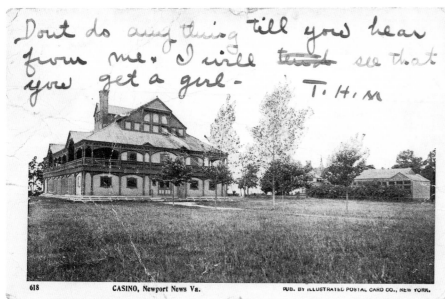

Don't do any thing till you hear from me. I will ~~~~ see that you get a girl — T. H. M

CASINO, Newport News Va.

Postmarked October 22, 1904.

The Casino, Grounds, and Pleasure Pavilion, Newport News, Va.

Postmarked May 5, 1913.

9171. CASINO PARK AND NEWPORT NEWS ACADEMY, NEWPORT NEWS, VA.

Postmarked May 11, 1908.

Casino Grounds, Newport News, Va.

Postmarked September 4, 1911.

Postmarked April 27, 1916.

Water front from Casino Grounds, showing C. & O. Piers, Newport News, Va

Lovers Walk, Casino Grounds,
C. & O. Coal Piers in distance, Newport News, Va.

Postmarked October 17, 1913.

Postmarked September 4, 1912.

Casino Pleasure Grounds,
Newport News, Va.

Hampton Roads showing the Harbor and Casino at Newport News, Va.

Postmarked
September 5, 1907.

11155   HAMPTON ROADS FROM HOTEL WARWICK, NEWPORT NEWS, VA.

564 BLOTTER   DELAYED WATER JUG   © F. A. S.

Schmelz National Bank
Newport News, Va.

The strongest Bank in the city. Ample security. Superior service. Four per cent on savings. : :

1918	JULY			1918		
SUN	MON	TUE	WED	THU	FRI	SAT
	1	2	3	4	5	6
7	8	9	10	11	12	13
14	15	16	17	18	19	20
21	22	23	24	25	26	27
28	29	30	31			

6244. JAMES RIVER FROM HOTEL WARWICK, NEWPORT NEWS, VA.   COPYRIGHT, 1902, BY DETROIT PHOTOGRAPHIC CO.

Bank blotter from Schmelz National Bank, 1918.

World War One

BOAT HARBOR, NEWPORT NEWS, VA.

Message on back: *Camp Stuart, Newport News, Virginia, January 9th 1919. Arrived here yesterday on board USS "Georgia." Will be back the last of the month.*

CURTISS AVIATION SCHOOL, SHOWING HYDROPLANE IN FLIGHT, NEWPORT NEWS, VA.

RETURNING TROOPS FROM OVER SEAS, NEWPORT NEWS, VA.

Postmarked August 20, 1920.

MEMORIAL ARCH, NEWPORT NEWS, VA.

Message on back: *Newport News, Virginia, May 22, 1919. Arrived here Wednesday morning from Bordeaux France on USS [illegible]. Arthur, USS Roanoke.*

Postmarked March 11, 1920.

HOTEL POCAHONTAS, NEWPORT NEWS, VA.

FIRST PRESBYTERIAN CHURCH, NEWPORT NEWS, VA.

Message on back: *January 5, 1919. Dear Mother, Just arrived in good old U.S.A. today and some glad to. Enjoyed the trip and am very well. We are having a nice little snow here tonight. The first fellow that I talked to here was from Harrisburg. I don't know how long I will be here but I think I will go to another camp. From Milton.*

Message on back: *Dear Shirley, Back in America. Arrived the 20th and expect to be in N.A. [North Attleboro, Mass.] soon. I am in a wonderful camp and living like a city class. K. Curtis. Postmarked March 23, 1919.*

128:—CHESAPEAKE AND OHIO TERMINAL, NEWPORT NEWS, VA.

48252

523:—Newport News Shipbuilding & Dry Dock Company, Newport News, Va.

45   NEWPORT NEWS SHIPBUILDING AND DRY DOCK CO., NEWPORT NEWS, VA.

4A142

7A-H340

Washington Avenue looking North, Newport News, Va.   1

119:-WASHINGTON AVENUE LOOKING NORTH, NEWPORT NEWS, VA.

47570

NN-134 Jefferson Avenue Looking North, Newport News, Va.

OB-H2223

NEWPORT NEWS HIGH SCHOOL, NEWPORT NEWS, VA.

PUBLIC LIBRARY AND MEDICAL ARTS BUILDING, NEWPORT NEWS, VA.

4A143

118:-NEW ARMORY, NEWPORT NEWS, VA.

47569

RIVERSIDE HOSPITAL   D-5431

Information on back: "Huntington Lodge, 5000 Huntington Avenue, Newport News, VA." Postmarked October 5, 1946.

TIDEWATER HOTEL — NEWPORT NEWS, VIRGINIA

Known All The World Over

1A2741

CRIGLER'S AUTO COURT. DIAL 2-9718, ROUTE 60, 6 MI. NORTH OF NEWPORT NEWS, VA.

NEAR YORKTOWN AND WILLIAMSBURG

½ MILE FROM MARINER'S MUSEUM

WARWICK HOTEL, NEWPORT NEWS, VA.

122886

THE COLONY INN   HILTON VILLAGE, VIRGINIA   MARY B. SHUMATE, MGR.

15—Colony Inn, Hilton Village, Newport News, Va.

115:-POST OFFICE AND WARWICK HOTEL, NEWPORT NEWS, VA.

47566

NEWPORT NEWS-JAMES RIVER BRIDGE

Information on back: "The Newport News-James River Bridge is one of the James River Bridge System, which is the longest in the world, leaping historic James River, at its mouth, four and one-half miles, connecting Hampton, Newport News, Norfolk, Portsmouth, Suffolk and the Virginia Peninsular and South Side. Has the largest lift span in existence, being three hundred feet wide, one hundred and fifty feet high, and weighs three million pounds. It was built in 1928 at a cost of six million dollars, and saves many hours of travel time in the Hampton Roads area. Crossing the bridge one has a complete view of the field of activities of the conflict between the Merrimac and the Monitor."

NEWPORT NEWS—JAMES RIVER BRIDGE, WORLD'S LONGEST HIGHWAY BRIDGE, (4½ MILES LONG)

4128-29

LOOKING NORTHWARD ACROSS THE JAMES RIVER

Postmarked September 22, 1930.

NEWPORT NEWS — JAMES RIVER BRIDGE, OF THE JAMES RIVER BRIDGE SYSTEM IN VIRGINIA

25,271 FT. LONG (FOUR AND ONE HALF MILES) PICTURE TAKEN BY U. S. A. AIR CORPS, LANGLEY FIELD, VA.

Postmarked October 9, 1936.

NN-135—New Pleasure Pier and James River Bridge, Newport News, Va.

2B-H1411

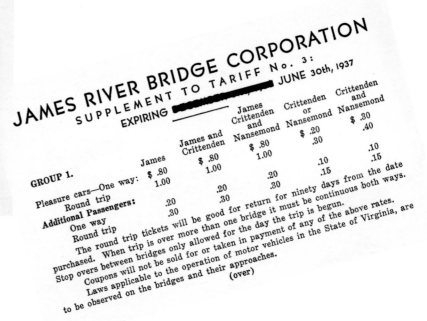

JAMES RIVER BRIDGE CORPORATION
SUPPLEMENT TO TARIFF No. 3:
EXPIRING ▬▬▬▬ JUNE 30th, 1937

GROUP 1.	James	James and Crittenden	James Crittenden and Nansemond	Crittenden or Nansemond	Crittenden and Nansemond
Pleasure cars—One way:	$ .80	$ .80	$ .80	$ .20	$ .30
Round trip	1.00	1.00	1.00	.30	.40
Additional Passengers:			.20	.10	.10
One way	.20	.20	.30	.15	.15
Round trip	.30	.30			

The round trip tickets will be good for return for ninety days from the date purchased. When trip is over more than one bridge it must be continuous both ways. Stop overs between bridges only allowed for the day the trip is begun. Coupons will not be sold for or taken in payment of any of the above rates. Laws applicable to the operation of motor vehicles in the State of Virginia, are to be observed on the bridges and their approaches.

(over)

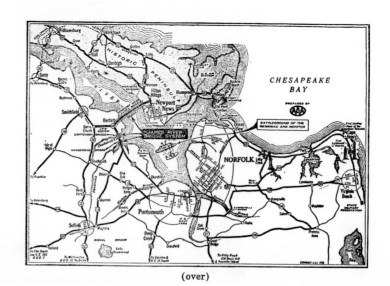

(over)

Views of
The Mariners' Museum
Newport News, Va.

PLACE
1½c
HERE

THE LIBRARY.

THE NORTH DISPLAY ROOM.

DISPLAY IN THE NORTHERN COLONNADE.

PALOS, BY SOROLLA.

VIEW OF THE DAM AND THE STATUE, LA JEUNESSE.

ENTRANCE TO THE MUSEUM SHOWING ANCHOR DISPLAY.

The Mariners' Museum, Newport News, Virginia.

Post card packet from the Mariners'
Museum, mid-1930.

MAIN ENTRANCE

MARINERS' MUSEUM, NEWPORT NEWS, VA.

7A-H338

80

139—Mariner's Museum, Newport News, Va.

6B-H546

Entrance to the Main Building of The Mariners' Museum—Statue of Leif Ericsson at Right

The Mariners' Museum, Newport News, Virginia

D-10149

Interior of Mariners' Museum, Newport News, Va.

8A-H3089

NN-149—Main Exhibit Room, Mariners' Museum, Newport News, Va.

2B-H1414

MAIN DISPLAY ROOM

CENTER DISPLAY ROOM

THE LIBRARY

SMALL BOAT DISPLAY

CITY RESERVOIR, NEWPORT NEWS, VA.

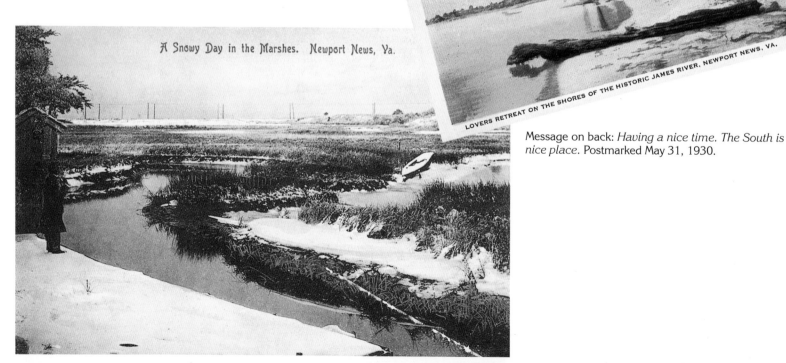

A Snowy Day in the Marshes. Newport News, Va.

LOVERS RETREAT ON THE SHORES OF THE HISTORIC JAMES RIVER, NEWPORT NEWS, VA.

Message on back: *Having a nice time. The South is a nice place.* Postmarked May 31, 1930.

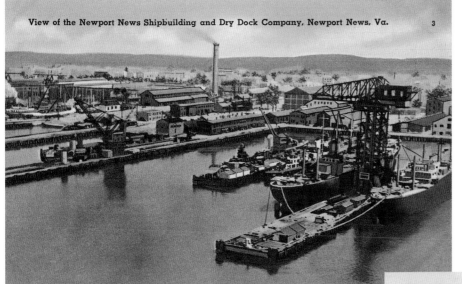

View of the Newport News Shipbuilding and Dry Dock Company, Newport News, Va. 3

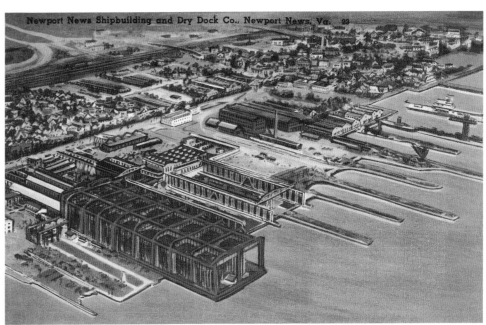

Newport News Shipbuilding and Dry Dock Co., Newport News, Va. 23

A prewar view of the shipyard, reprinted and censored during the War years.

6— Newport News Shipbuilding and Dry Dock Co., Newport News, Va.

PHOTO COURTESY FAIRCHILD AERIAL SURVEYS, INC.

8A-H3090

4A-H1641

Information on back: "Travel by Ferry across Hampton Roads and see Colonial Williamsburg and historic Yorktown via Norfolk-Newport News or Norfolk-Old Point Routes. Fast schedules, lunch rooms and rest rooms on all steamers."

NK-22—Ferry Steamer "Hampton Roads", Norfolk-Newport News Ferry Route Across Hampton Roads

9A-H567

NN-153—Newport News and Norfolk Ferry Pier and W. G. H. Broadcasting Station, Newport News, Va.

Naval and Military Club, Newport News, Va.

CATHOLIC MARITIME CLUB ● NEWPORT NEWS, VIRGINIA

The Catholic Maritime Club served the Merchant Marine sailors.

A RENTAL OFFICE, ONE OF FOUR, COPELAND PARK, FEDERAL PUBLIC HOUSING AUTHORITY,

NEWPORT NEWS, VIRGINIA   E-6809

Postmarked October 7, 1948.

No. 710   HOMEWARD-BOUND, CAMP PATRICK HENRY, VA.

Information on back: "The 469th Army Service Force Band marches under the "Victory Arch" at Camp Patrick Henry as it leads a column of debarks, fresh from the European Theatre of Operations, out of the camp on their way home for furlough."

No. 719   TELEPHONE CENTER, CAMP PATRICK HENRY, VA.

Information on back: "The Telephone Center in Area No. 6, one of the most popular and sought-after buildings at Camp Patrick Henry, where men come in crowds to make calls to their families at home."

No. 718   HEADQUARTERS, CAMP PATRICK HENRY, VA.

Information on back: "Camp Patrick Henry's headquarters building located in the center of 1700 acres of thick woodland, where the activities of the staging area are directed. The camp, often referred to as a 'Sylvan Glen,' is run by the Transportation Corps of the Army Service Forces."

COSMETICS

THE GENERAL STORE, CAMP PATRICK HENRY, VA.

No. 716

Information on back: "The Main Exchange, commonly known as 'The General Store,' is shown in action at Camp Patrick Henry. Here, a home-hungry GI can satisfy his wants as he roams around an Army department store."

No. 714   INTERIOR OF "LAST CHANCE" NIGHT CLUB, CAMP PATRICK HENRY, VA.

Information on back: "The interior of Camp Patrick Henry's favorite night spot, the 'Last Chance' Night Club, is shown here. The renovated recreation hall affords old-time waiters and cigarette girls, eager to serve the returning debarks. The photo shows the stage and the band stand in the right forward."

Information on back: "'The Last Chance' Night Club at Camp Patrick Henry, fashioned after an old-time Western Saloon, is the Staging Area's most popular night spot."

No. 713   "LAST CHANCE" NIGHT CLUB, CAMP PATRICK HENRY, VA.

PHOTO VA. STATE CHAMBER   9A-H1519

Aerial View of Newport News, Va., on Hampton Roads   15

RR STATION

Courtyard showing Japanese salvage submarine

The Mariners' Museum, Newport News, Virginia

D-10134

NN-131—Beautiful Homes on Huntington Avenue, Newport News, Va.

OB-H2221

Message on back: *I certainly do see plenty of soldiers, sailors & everything down here. Having a swelligant time. Lorna.* Post-marked July 31, 1941.

60:-VIEW OF JAMES RIVER AND BRIDGE FROM MARINER'S MUSEUM GROUNDS AT NIGHT. NEWPORT NEWS. VA.

46231

NN-138— Aerial View of Entrance and Lake, Mariner's Museum, Newport News, Va.

PHOTO

9A-H1520

2—View of Swan and Lake at Mariners Museum, Newport News, Va.

9A-H2127

93

Memorial to Collis P. Huntington in the Museum Park
by Anna Hyatt Huntington

The Mariners' Museum, Newport News, Virginia

NN101—Courthouse and Public Safety Building
Newport, News, Va.

NN-151—Interior Exhibit, the Memorial Museum of the American Legion, Newport News, Va.

2B-H1412

Tidewater Hotel
Newport News, Va.

"Happyland" TOURIST HAVEN, INC.

5 Miles North of Newport News on U.S. 168

Section of Main Dining Room, NEW WARWICK HOTEL, Newport News, Va.

1107-30

Postmarked September 17, 1906.

Postmarked November 11, 1905.

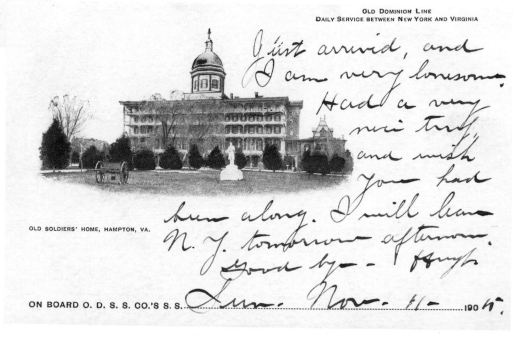

Postmarked March 27, 1919.

Postmarked December 29, 1906.

97

Hampton Institute Battalion   Reviewed by Marshal Petain and General Pershing

Old Dominion Line
Daily Service between
New York and Virginia

Hampton Institute, Hampton, Va.

ON BOARD O. D. S. s. CO.'S S. S. 190

H5—Clock Tower of Memorial Church
Hampton Institute
Hampton, Va.

OLD DOMINION LINE
DAILY SERVICE BETWEEN NEW YORK AND VIRGINIA

BIRDS-EYE VIEW OF HAMPTON, VA.

ON BOARD O. D S. S. CO.'S S. S. ————————————————————————— 190

3031—A Pile of James River Oyster Shells, Hampton, Va.

NN-120—Business Section and Apartments, Kecoughtan, Hampton, Va.

Between Hampton and Newport News, Va.

2B-H1409

Postmarked July 7, 1943.

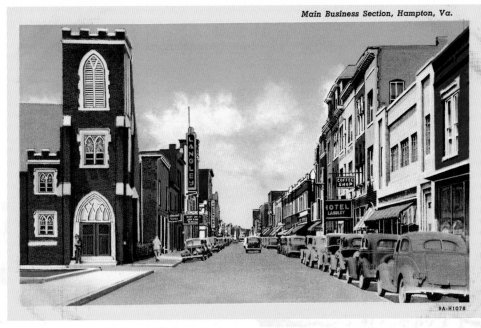

Main Business Section, Hampton, Va.

9A-H1078

P-300—Mellon Street, Phoebus, Va. Main Boulevard of Newport News and Old Point Comfort

9A-H1083

2—Queen Street Looking East, Hampton, Va.

OB-H2216

5—Hotel Langley and Apartments, Hampton, Va.

Sea Food Industry, Hampton, Va.

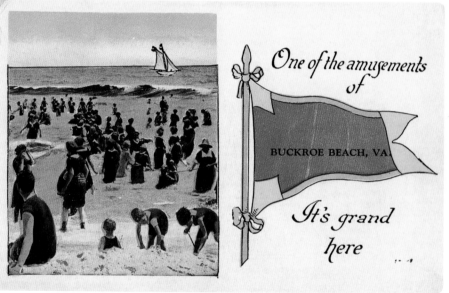

Generic postcard. Postmarked May 20, 1916.

BATH HOUSE, BUCKROE BEACH, VA.

Postmarked July 30, 1915.

HOTEL LAWN AND BATH HOUSE, BUCKROE BEACH, VA.

PAVILION AND HOTEL, BY NIGHT, BUCKROE BEACH, VA.

38284

Postmarked July 31, 1931.

Buckroe Beach Hotel, Buckroe Beach, Va.

BATHING BEACH, BUCKROE BEACH, VA.

Postmarked July 18, 1924.

Information on back: "Gordon's Cottage Court, Your Home Away From Home, Buckroe Beach, Virginia. Completely furnished cottages with tile bath, furnished kitchen, hot water, linens and towels. Located just one block from swimming beach. Phone: Hampton 4771."

Gordon's Cottage Court, Buckroe Beach, Virginia

Bird's-Eye View of Amusement Park and Chesapeake Bay, Buckroe Beach, Va.

9A-H1518

Information on back: "The Chesapeake Bay area of Virginia has numerous shore resorts. Buckroe Beach is one of the largest popular bathing beaches. The Amusement Park is excellent and has a beautiful dance pavilion."

B-175—Bird's-Eye View looking South across Chesapeake Bay, Buckroe Beach, Va.

9A-H1517

Information on back: "A beautiful view. Nearby is scene of famous battle between Monitor and Merrimac, first ironclad. One of the most historic resort areas in America."

Old Point Comfort:

The Chamberlin Hotel & Fort Monroe

S 39 Hotel Chamberlin, Ft. Monroe Va.

The Chamberlin Hotel opened at Old Point Comfort in 1896 as one of the most luxurious hotels in the United States. Burned to the ground in 1920, it reopened as The Chamberlin –Vanderbilt Hotel on April 1, 1928 . Message on back: *July 19, 1909. Our first stop on our trip south. Just as good as it looks. With love, Richard.*

Postmarked April 15, 1906.

OLD POINT COMFORT, Va. Chamberlin Hotel.

Information on back: "The Chamberlin Hotel at Old Point Comfort is noted for its size, beauty of location, superb architectural arrangements, and furnishings of princely lavishness; it is equipped with every convenience and appliance. The main dining-room is in the form of a Greek cross, having an endless number of windows and seating 500 guests; its ball and palm rooms are exquisitely furnished, and has a spacious glass veranda overlooking the area."

HOTEL CHAMBERLIN, OLD POINT COMFORT, VA.   4/15/06.

A-12 ILLUSTRATED POST CARD CO., N. Y.

Do you remember

70267 THE SEA WALL, OLD POINT COMFORT, VA.

Postmarked April 13, 1908.

9158. HOTEL CHAMBERLIN, OLD POINT COMFORT, VA.

3017—Hotel Chamberlain, Old Point Comfort, Va.

EAST FRONT

HOTEL CHAMBERLIN

GEO. F. ADAMS, MGR.

FORTRESS MONROE, VA.

BAND CONCERT

HOTEL CHAMBERLIN, OLD POINT COMFORT, VA.

FORT MONROE GARRISON ON PARADE, OLD POINT COMFORT, VA.

Information on back: "Chamberlin Hotel, Old Point Comfort, VA. This world famous hotel, luxurious in the extreme, is always graced with a social strata that ranks exceedingly high. Is beautifully situated close to Fortress Monroe and overlooks Historical Hampton Roads."

Advertising overprint.

Front of advertising overprint postcard, postmarked May 26, 1914.

Back of advertising overprint postcard, postmarked May 26, 1914.

Chamberlain Hotel, Old Point, Va.

13168. View from Chamberlain Hotel Veranda, Old Point Comfort, Va.

Message on back: *May 5, 1915. Do not know where all these people came from, have not seen them since we have been here. Our room is in about the middle of the picture on the 2nd floor. There are 17 battleships in front of us tonight. We ought to be well protected. All well, expect to be home the first of the week. Herbert.*

RECEPTION ROOM

ELECTRIC LIGHT CABINETS

MASSAGE ROOM

BATH PERAMBULATOR

HOTEL CHAMBERLIN
GEO. F. ADAMS, MGR.
FORTRESS MONROE, VA.

HYDROTHERAPEUTIC BATHS, HOTEL CHAMBERLIN, THE MOST COMPLETE ESTABLISHMENT IN AMERICA

HOTEL CHAMBERLIN   GEO. F. ADAMS, MGR.   FORTRESS MONROE, VA.

Chamberlin Touring Yacht "Osprey"	*Descriptive Folders and Tickets at Hotel Office*	Chamberlin Sight Seeing Auto
Daily--9:30 a.m. 2:30 p.m. Delightful Sail of 3 Hours, over Hampton Roads $1.00	## Noonday Meal	Hampton Soldiers' Home Fort Monroe Every Day at 10:00 a. m. and 2:30 p. m. $1.00

Noonday Meal

YORK RIVER OYSTERS COCKTAIL   LITTLE NECK CLAMS

HOME MADE VEGETABLE SOUP   CONSOMME, HOT OR COLD

PICKLED FIGS   GREEN ONIONS   SLICED CUCUMBERS

BROILED SPANISH MACKEREL, MAITRE D'HOTEL
POTATOES, HASHED IN CREAM

CURRY OF OYSTERS A L'INDIENNE

SPRING LAMB, SAUTE, WITH FRENCH PEAS

ROAST HAM, CHAMPAGNE SAUCE

BOILED AND MASHED POTATOES   FRIED EGG PLANT
STEAMED RICE

CHICKEN SALAD   PICKLED OYSTERS   COLD SLAW
ENDIVE AND TOMATO SALAD

COLD ROAST BEEF   LAMB   TURKEY   HAM   ITALIAN SALAMI
KIELER SPROTTEN   CORNED BEEF   HEAD CHEESE
PICKLED LAMB'S TONGUE   BOSTON BAKED BEANS   SMOKED OX TONGUE
HOT OR COLD DEVILLED CRABS

VIRGINIA CORN BREAD   **WHITE CROSS BUTTERMILK**   HOT GINGERBREAD

WHEAT GRIDDLE CAKES WITH MAPLE SYRUP

BLUEBERRY PIE   ASSORTED CAKE
LEMON SHERBET

PRESERVED STRAWBERRIES   DAMSON PRESERVE
BAKED APPLE WITH CREAM

SALTINE WAFERS   WATER CRACKERS
CREAM, ROQUEFORT AND AMERICAN CHEESE

COFFEE

DISTILLED WATER USED EXCLUSIVELY

TEA WILL BE SERVED IN THE PALM GARDEN FROM 5:00 TO 6:00 P. M

MONDAY, MARCH 27, 1911

☞ If Menu Card is mailed with Post Card and any writing placed thereon, postage will be 2 cts.

Chamberlin Hotel Luncheon Menu for March 27, 1911. The top third of the menu detaches to form a postcard, one of a series of 25 postcard views of the Chamberlin and Fortress Monroe.

CHAMBERLIN-VANDERBILT HOTEL,
OLD POINT COMFORT,
NEAR NORFOLK, VA.—33

BOAT LANDING, OLD POINT COMFORT, VA.

Message on back: *Greetings. Hows the battle works. Its swell to be loafing (and can I loaf). The flowers here are gorgeous. Magnolias and gardenias are just everywhere. They carry them around in buckets here. Some stuff, eh! La-Vern.* Postmarked June 6, 1935

HAMPTON ROADS, VA.

Information on back: "Hampton Roads. Hampton Roads is the broad and celebrated stretch of water in front of Old Point Comfort and Fortress Monroe. It presents one of the most varied and animated scenes of maritime life, and is a favorite rendezvous for the ships of the Navy."

115

Information on back: "Panoramic View. Fort Monroe was established on its present site in 1817, but as far back as 1630, a fort existed near the mouth of the James River. The present fort has passed through many changes, and is now equipped with the most modern guns and conceded to be the best fortified position in America." Message on back: *Here till our money is gone. W&F.* Postmarked July 27, 1908.

FORT MONROE, VA. Panoramic View.

9347 FORT MONROE OLD POINT COMFORT VA

COPYRIGHT, 1905, BY DETROIT PUBLISHING CO

Dear Annie - I send you the above. Wishing you a Merry Xmas & a happy New Year. Your friend Mr J.C. Smith

am at Old Pt. Comfort, seeing the big
fleet. Lots to tell you when I get home

Postmarked March 6, 1909.

Fortress Monroe, Va. Main Gate.

Postmarked May 9, 1909.

Old Dominion Line
Daily Service
between New York
and Virginia

View at Old
Point Comfort, Va.

ON BOARD O. D. S. S. CO.'S S. S. ————— 190

70273 CASEMENT WHERE JEFFERSON DAVIS WAS IMPRISONED, FORTRESS MONROE VA   COPR. DETROIT PUBLISHING CO.

Wharf at Old Point, Va.

Jackies Landing at Old Point Comfort, Va.

U. S. BATTLESHIP FLEET BY NIGHT, HAMPTON ROADS, OLD POINT COMFORT, VA.

VIRGINIA

The roses nowhere bloom so white
 As in Virginia,
The sunshine nowhere shines so bright
 As in Virginia.
The birds sing nowhere quite so sweet
 And nowhere hearts so lightly beat,
For Heaven and Earth both seem to meet
 Down in Virginia.

The days are never quite so long
 As in Virginia;
Nor quite as filled with happy song,
 As in Virginia;
And when my time has come to die,
 Just take me back and let me lie
Close to the Blue Ridge Mountains High
 Down in Virginia.

There is nowhere a land so fair
 As in Virginia,
So full of song, so free of care,
 As in Virginia.
And I believe that happy land
 The Lord's prepared for mortal man,
Is built exactly on the plan
 Of Old Virginia.

12-INCH MORTARS IN ACTION AT FORTRESS MONROE, VA.

Information on back: "Mortars in Action, Fortress Monroe, VA. One of the most interesting sights at this fortification is the firing of the mortars at various times. The projectiles in their flight through the air can be plainly seen with the naked eye."

HYGEIA HOTEL, OLD POINT COMFORT, VA.

6251. COPYRIGHT, 1902, BY DETROIT PHOTOGRAPHIC CO,

HYGEIA HOTEL.
OLD POINT COMFORT. VA.

Arthur Livingston, Publisher, New York. 337

Old Dominion Liner landing at Old Point Comfort, Va.

A very rare view showing the old Chamberlin Hotel and the Hygeia Hotel. The Hygeia was the first hotel at Fortress Monroe, opening in 1820. It moved to a location near the steamboat wharf in 1863, reopened as a restaurant, and enlarged to a hotel in 1872. The large wooden structure became a popular destination until it was bought by the Chamberlin and razed in 1902. The two stood together only six years. Postmarked August 29, 1901.

SHERWOOD INN, OLD POINT COMFORT, VA.

Information on back: "Sherwood Inn, Old Point Comfort, VA. (Fortress Monroe) This hotel, situated at Old Point Comfort offers excellent services at moderate rates. It adjoins Fortress Monroe, where can be seen the daily drill of Soldier Life and other interesting attractions adjoining this government reservation."

Advertising overprint postcard for the Jamestown Exposition.

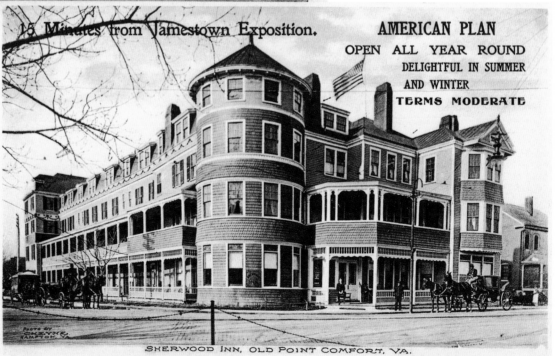

15 Minutes from Jamestown Exposition.

AMERICAN PLAN
OPEN ALL YEAR ROUND
DELIGHTFUL IN SUMMER
AND WINTER
TERMS MODERATE

SHERWOOD INN, OLD POINT COMFORT, VA.

Opposite Main Entrance of Fort Monroe   J. G. TAYLOR, Manager

YORKTOWN, Va. Main Street.

Information on back: "Main Street. The village of Yorktown is in many respects the most important historic locality of the Revolutionary War. It was here that the war came to a close with the surrender of Lord Cornwallis and the British troops to Gen. George Washington and the Continental Army, together with their French Allies. Yorktown remains to-day almost exactly as it appeared a century and a quarter ago."

THE HARBOR, YORKTOWN, VA.

6695. COPYRIGHT, 1903, BY DETROIT PHOTOGRAPHIC CO.

10512. A STREET IN YORKTOWN, VA.

OLDEST HOUSE IN YORKTOWN AND NELSON HOUSE, YORKTOWN, VA.

Postmarked October 3, 1909.

6693   FIRST CUSTOM HOUSE IN AMERICA, YORKTOWN, VA.

Old Point, Va.

Reached here Friday morning Turner

OLD ENGLISH TAVERN, BUILT IN 1725, YORKTOWN, VA.

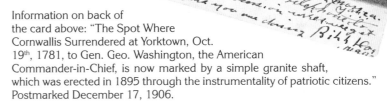

YORKTOWN, Va, Spot Where Cornwallis Surrendered.

Information on back of
the card above: "The Spot Where
Cornwallis Surrendered at Yorktown, Oct.
19th, 1781, to Gen. Geo. Washington, the American
Commander-in-Chief, is now marked by a simple granite shaft,
which was erected in 1895 through the instrumentality of patriotic citizens."
Postmarked December 17, 1906.

7847. HOUSE WHERE CORNWALLIS SURRENDERED, YORKTOWN, VA. COPYRIGHT, 1905, BY DETROIT PHOTOGRAPHO CO.

Postmarked October 27, 1905.

Postmarked May 21, 1907.

Cornwallis, Hiding Place, Yorktown, Va.

DUKE OF GLOUCESTER STREET, WILLIAMSBURG, VA.

COLONIAL RESTAURANT
The Home of Famous Food
Williamsburg, Virginia

5813

Williamsburg Lodge, Williamsburg, Virginia

COLONIAL RESTAURANT
The Home of Famous Food
Williamsburg, Virginia

5814

Benns Church, SMITHFIELD, Va.   3069.

Old St. Luke's Church, Built in 1632, Isle of Wight, Va.

Genuine Smithfield, Virginia, Hams come from Peanut Fed Hogs   71649

Genuine Smithfield, Virginia, Hams in Dry Salt Process   71650

Would you like to write a book?

For over thirty years we have had the privilege and pleasure of meeting hundreds of people with wonderful ideas for new books. For many of them, writing a book was only a far off dream, something they hoped to do someday. With our encouragement they went on to produce a beautiful, useful addition to the literature in their field.

If you are one of those people who always dreamed of writing a book, we would love to hear from you. New ideas and authors are the lifeblood of what we do here. We have gathered together a team of people who will do everything they can to make the concept of a book become a reality.

We are eagerly seeking authors to write illustrated, regional history books. With vintage photographs and postcards these big, 11" x 8-1/2" books are bringing bygone eras back to life. Illustrated in glorious full color, each book is stunning & unique.

The following form has helped hundreds to gather their thoughts and begin the process of compiling a book. Submit your idea to us in one of the following ways:

• Email the following information to info@schifferbooks.com

• Copy and mail this form to Acquisitions, Schiffer Publishing, Ltd. 4880 Lower Valley Rd., Atglen, PA 19310

• Fax us at 610-593-2002

We look forward to hearing from you!

Name _____

Street Address

_____

_____

_____

Home Phone _____

Work Phone _____

Fax _____

Email address: _____

Website: _____

Best time to call: _____

The subject of the book you are proposing: _____

_____

_____

_____

Your background in the field: _____

_____

_____

_____

_____

The number of postcards/historic images you own or have access to: _____

A description of your target audience, i.e. population, relevant organizations, etc.: _____

_____

_____

_____

_____

Specific retailers who would carry your book:

_____

_____

_____

_____

_____

_____

_____

_____

Media that would review/promote your book:

_____

_____

_____

_____

Schiffer Publishing, Ltd.
4880 Lower Valley Road
Atglen, PA 19310
610-593-1777
www.schifferbooks.com